LOOK IT UP
Now in a fully revised edition
1. You and Your Body
2. People and Customs
3. What People Do
4. The Prehistoric World
5. Ships and Boats
6. People of Long Ago
7. The Sea
8. The Earth
9. Cold-Blooded Animals
10. Warm-Blooded Animals
11. Sport and Entertainment
12. The World of Machines
13. Land Travel
14. Flying
15. Outer Space
16. Index

Photo Credits: Aerofilms; B.&C.Alexander; Heather Angel, M.Sc.,F.R.P.S.; Australian News and Information Bureau; J. Allan Cash; Robert Estall; Michael Holford; Mats Wibe Lund Jr.; Dick Makin; Photri; Picturepoint; R.K.Pilsbury; Ronald Sheridan; Spectrum; Swiss National Tourist Office; John Topham; ZEFA.

Front cover: Heather Angel/Biofotos.

Illustrators: Gill Embleton; Dan Escott; Elizabeth Graham-Yool; Giles Hollingsworth; Illustra; Eric Jewell; Ben Manchipp; Stephanie Manchipp; John Marshall; Raymond Turvey; Roger Walker; Mike Whelply.

First edition © Macmillan Publishers Limited, 1979
Reprinted in 1981, 1982, 1983 and 1984
Second edition © Macmillan Publishers Limited, 1985

All rights reserved. No reproduction, copy or transmission of this publication in any form or by any means, may be made without written permission

Chief Educational Adviser
Lynda Snowdon

Teacher Advisory Panel
Helen Craddock, John Enticknap, Arthur Razzell

Editorial Board
Jan Burgess, Rosemary Canter, Philip M. Clark, Beatrice Phillpotts, Sue Seddon, Philip Steele

Picture Researchers
Caroline Adams, Anne Marie Ehrlich, Gayle Hayter, Ethel Hurwicz, Pat Hodgson, Stella Martin, Frances Middlestorb

Designer
Keith Faulkner

Contributors and consultants
John E. Allen, Neil Ardley, Sue Becklake, Robert Burton, Barry Cox, Jacqueline Dineen, David J. Fletcher, Plantagenet Somerset Fry, Bill Gunston, Robin Kerrod, Mark Lambert, Anne Millard, Kaye Orten, Ian Ridpath, Peter Stephens, Nigel Swann, Aubrey Tulley, Tom Williamson, Thomas Wright

Published by Macmillan Children's Books
a division of Macmillan Publishers Limited
4 Little Essex Street, London WC2R 3LF
Associated companies throughout the world

ISBN 0 333 39726 6 (volume 8)
ISBN 0 333 39568 9 (complete set)

Printed in Hong Kong

The Earth

Second Edition
LOOK IT UP

Contents

	Page
PLANET EARTH	4
The turning earth	6
INSIDE THE EARTH	8
Earthquakes	10
Volcanoes	12
Rocks	14
Minerals	16
Mining	18
Oil	20
THE ATMOSPHERE	22
The water cycle	24
Winds	26
Clouds and rain	28
Snow	30
Thunderstorms and rainbows	32
Watching the weather	34
Living in different climates	36

	Page
THE FACE OF THE EARTH	**38**
Mountains	**40**
Rivers and streams	**42**
Lakes and waterfalls	**44**
Caves	**46**
VARIED LANDSCAPES	**48**
Tropical rain forests	**50**
Grasslands	**52**
Hot deserts	**54**
Broad-leaved forests	**56**
Coniferous forests	**58**
Tundra and ice	**60**
Spoiled land	**62**
DID YOU KNOW?	**64**
INDEX	

PLANET EARTH

The earth we live on is a huge ball of rock circling around the sun. Much of the earth is covered by water. This picture shows what the earth looks like from the moon. You can see the sea and land below the clouds. Round the earth is a layer of air called the atmosphere.

The turning earth

As the earth travels around the sun it also spins like a top. The earth turns round once every 24 hours.
When the place where you live faces the sun, it is day. Then, as your side of the earth turns away from the sun, it becomes night. It is darkest at midnight, when you are facing directly away from the sun.

When it is midday in New York it is nearly midnight in Hong Kong, on the other side of the world.

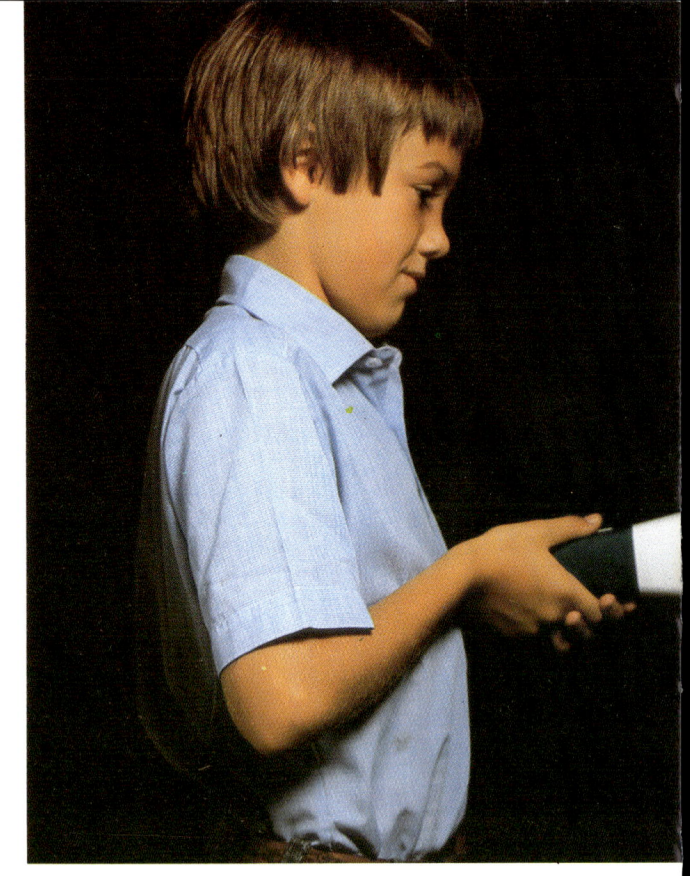

**New York
midday**

You can show how the earth moves from day to night by shining a bright torch on to a globe.

Pretend the torch is the sun. Mark where you live on the globe and ask someone to turn the globe round. You will see that when it is night where you live, it is daytime on the other side of the world.

When it is midnight in New York it is nearly midday in Hong Kong.

New York
midnight

INSIDE THE EARTH

If you could take the earth to pieces, you would see the different layers inside. The centre of the earth is called the core. It is made of very hot liquid metal. Round the core is a layer of rock called the mantle. This rock is like thick hot syrup. The outside layer, or crust, is much cooler than the other layers.

The core and mantle of the earth are very thick. The crust is much thinner. The layer of crust round the earth is like this thin layer of paint round the ball.

The earth's crust is thicker in some places than in others. Where the crust is very thick, it sticks up above the level of the sea. These thick parts are the land.

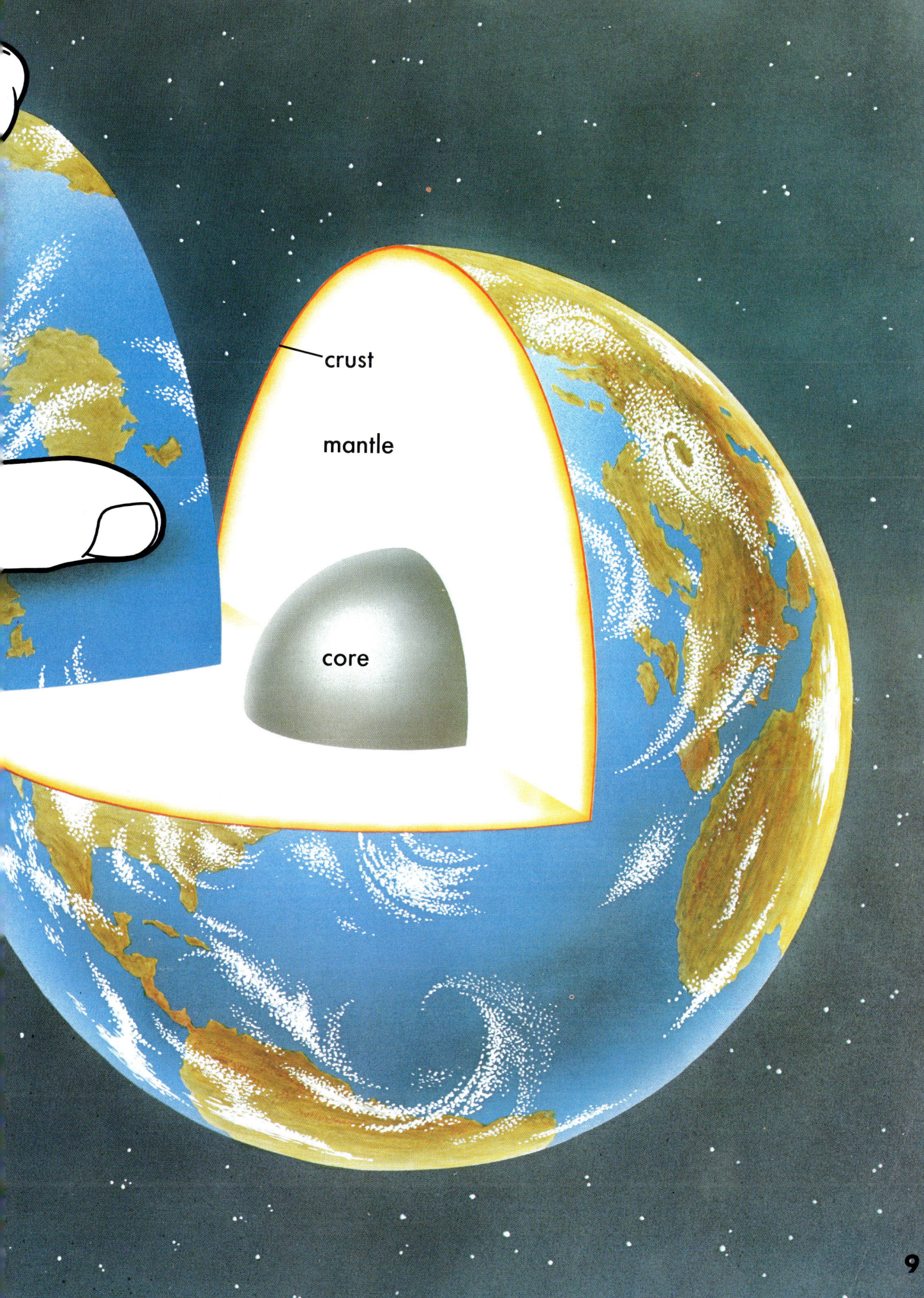

Earthquakes

Inside the earth, the hot syrupy rock below the crust is always moving about. This movement has made huge cracks in the crust. Sometimes the movement from below makes one large piece of land slip against another piece of land. When this happens the ground trembles. There is an earthquake.

Sometimes a block of land slips below the land next to it. The crack between the two blocks of land is called a fault.

At other times a block of land slips sideways along a fault. There are many faults in the earth's crust.

In places where earthquakes are likely to happen, low wooden houses are better than brick or stone houses. They do not fall down so easily. The picture on the left shows what happened in a big earthquake in Alaska. The earth shook and big cracks opened up in the ground. Even the wooden houses fell down.

These tall buildings in Italy have been badly damaged by an earthquake. Some have collapsed into piles of bricks and rubble.

Volcanoes

Sometimes hot liquid rock below the crust is forced up to the surface through a crack to form a volcano. There is a lot of gas in the liquid rock. When it reaches the surface the gas escapes. Pieces of red hot liquid rock shoot high into the air. This rock is called lava. The lava cools and falls to the ground.

This volcano erupted in Iceland in 1973. Fountains of red hot lava shot into the air. Bits of lava fell all round, and buried some houses.

In the big picture you can see the hot lava inside a volcano. Some lava is pouring out of the crater at the top.

13

Rocks

Rocks are formed in many different ways. Basalt is a kind of lava that comes from volcanoes. Shale is made of hardened mud and limestone is usually made of tiny seashells. Shale and limestone were formed long ago at the bottom of the sea. Movements of the earth's crust have pushed them up as land.

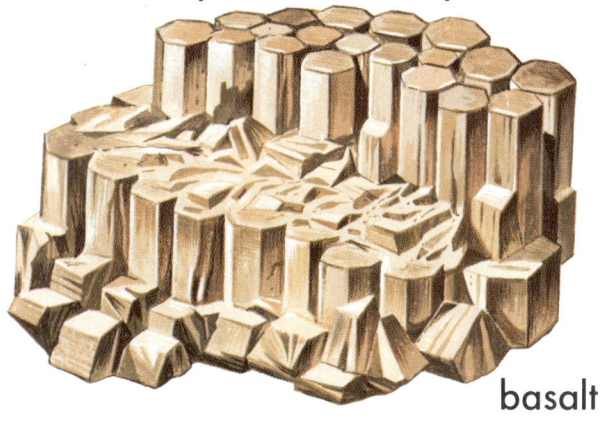
basalt

shale

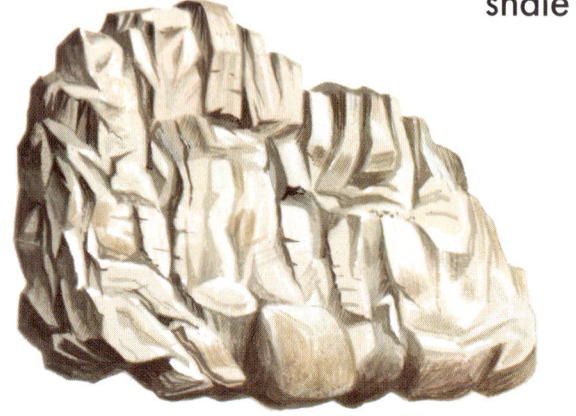
limestone

This huge statue of an Egyptian king was made of sandstone. It was carved thousands of years ago.

These sandstone rocks formed millions of years ago. Sandstone rocks are made of tiny sand grains that have stuck together.

This famous marble building is called the Parthenon. It is in Greece. Marble is a hard rock. It is often used to decorate important buildings and to make sculptures.

Huge blocks of marble are being cut out of this hillside. Marble is limestone that has been heated and squeezed inside the earth.

Granite is another very hard rock. This church is built of granite. It is in Salt Lake City, in America.

This is a granite quarry. The granite was formed millions of years ago when hot liquid rock slowly cooled deep inside the earth's crust

Minerals

The rocks of the earth's crust are made up of many different kinds of mineral. These pictures show a few of these minerals and how they are used. You will see that some of the minerals, like diamonds and quartz, are divided into many pieces. These are called crystals. Crystals of one mineral are usually the same shape.

diamonds

Diamond crystals are very hard. They are used to drill holes and to make needles for record players.

bauxite

Bauxite is a brown mineral which is easily found. It contains aluminium, which is a useful lightweight metal. Kettles and saucepans are often made of aluminium.

asbestos

Asbestos crystals are long thin fibres. These fibres do not burn, so asbestos is used to make fire-proof clothes for firemen.

gold

Gold is a precious yellow metal. It was once used to make coins. Gold is very expensive because it is so difficult to find.

Each of the minerals in rocks formed in a different way. Diamonds formed deep in the earth's mantle. They were carried up to the surface through cracks in the crust. Bauxite formed on the earth's surface in places where it was hot and wet. Quartz formed when hot liquid rock cooled deep in the earth's crust.

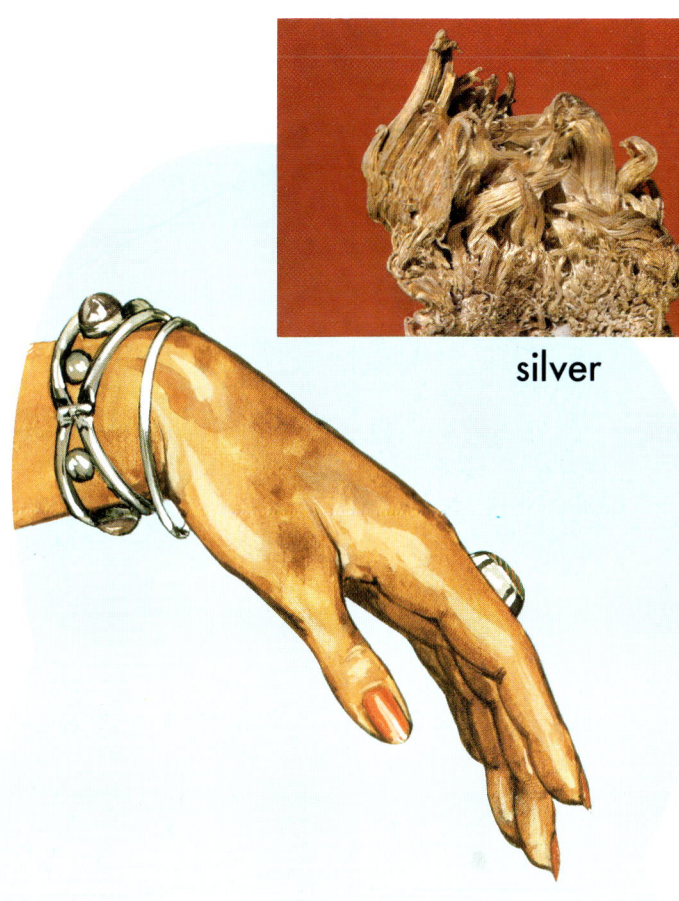
silver

quartz

Quartz usually has long clear crystals which are very big. Quartz crystals are used in clocks and watches to keep the time.

Silver is a precious metal. When silver is polished, it looks very attractive. It is used to make bracelets and other jewellery.

Mining

Some rocks contain useful metals. These rocks are called ores. In other rocks there are layers of coal or other useful materials like salt and asbestos. Sometimes miners can dig the ore or coal from the surface of the earth. When the ore or coal lies deep in the earth, it has to be brought up from underground.

The picture above shows a copper mine in Tasmania.

The picture on the right shows a coal mine. The miners need fresh air to breathe underground. The arrows show where fresh air is pumped in and stale air is pumped out.

18

These miners are working in an underground coal mine. Coal is made up of the remains of plants that lived millions of years ago. When the plants died, their remains were buried under mud and sand. Over the ages these remains were squeezed until they formed coal.

In some places tiny bits of gold collect in streams. These people are looking for gold.

Oil

Oil began as the remains of tiny sea creatures that lived millions of years ago. Slowly their remains were squeezed and heated in the earth until they turned into oil. Oil took a very long time to form, but now people are using it up very quickly. Soon there may be very little oil left.

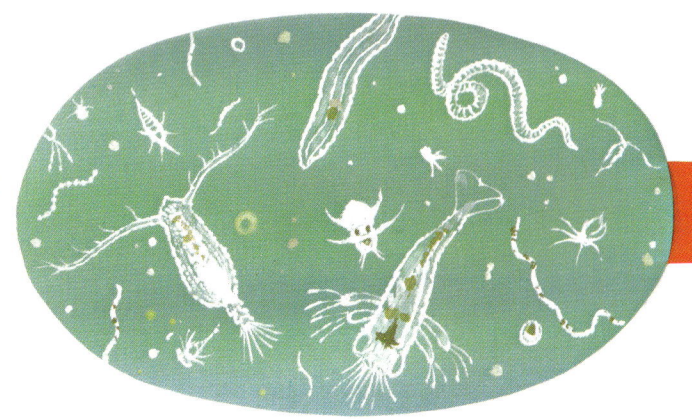

These tiny sea creatures lived millions of years ago. They have been drawn bigger than they were.

The oil is piped to the shore. It is stored in a building called a terminal.

If there is enough oil in the trap, a ship lays a pipeline from the trap to the shore.

The oil is pumped into an oil tanker. The tanker takes the oil to a place called an oil refinery.

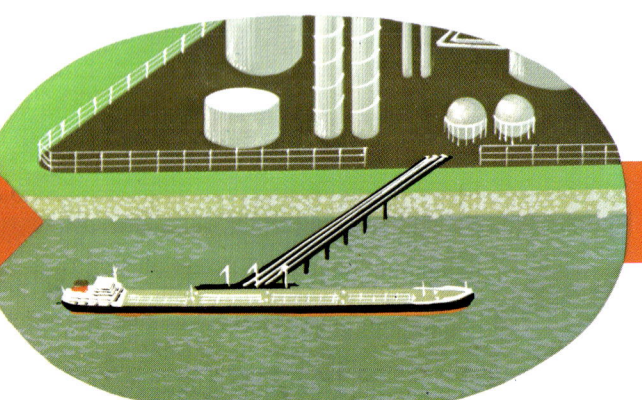

In the refinery, oil is separated into different types. Some are used to make plastics and chemicals.

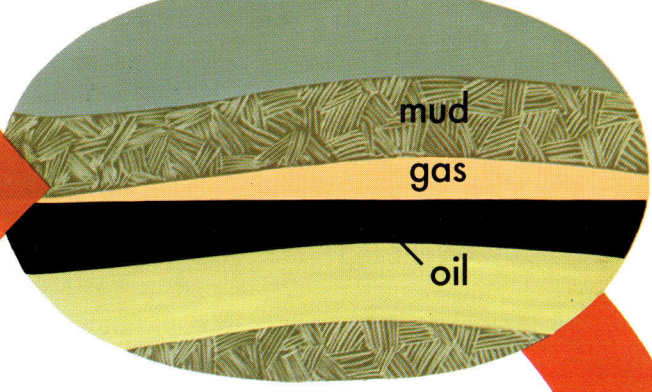

The creatures were buried by mud on the sea floor. After millions of years, they turned into oil and gas.

The oil and gas moved upwards and became trapped under layers of hard mud.

A hole is drilled into the sea bed to find out how much oil is in a trap. The drills go a long way down.

Today, scientists in ships use special equipment to find oil trapped beneath the sea.

Some oil is used to make petrol. The petrol is taken in petrol tankers to garages.

At the garage, the petrol is stored in underground tanks. Pumps feed the petrol into cars.

THE ATMOSPHERE

The atmosphere is the layer of air that surrounds the earth. Air is a mixture of different gases. These gases include oxygen and water vapour. As you go higher up in the atmosphere there is less oxygen. It becomes much harder to breathe. When people climb very high mountains they take extra oxygen with them to help them to breathe. In this picture you can see how high birds and aircraft fly.

jumbo jet 15,000 metres

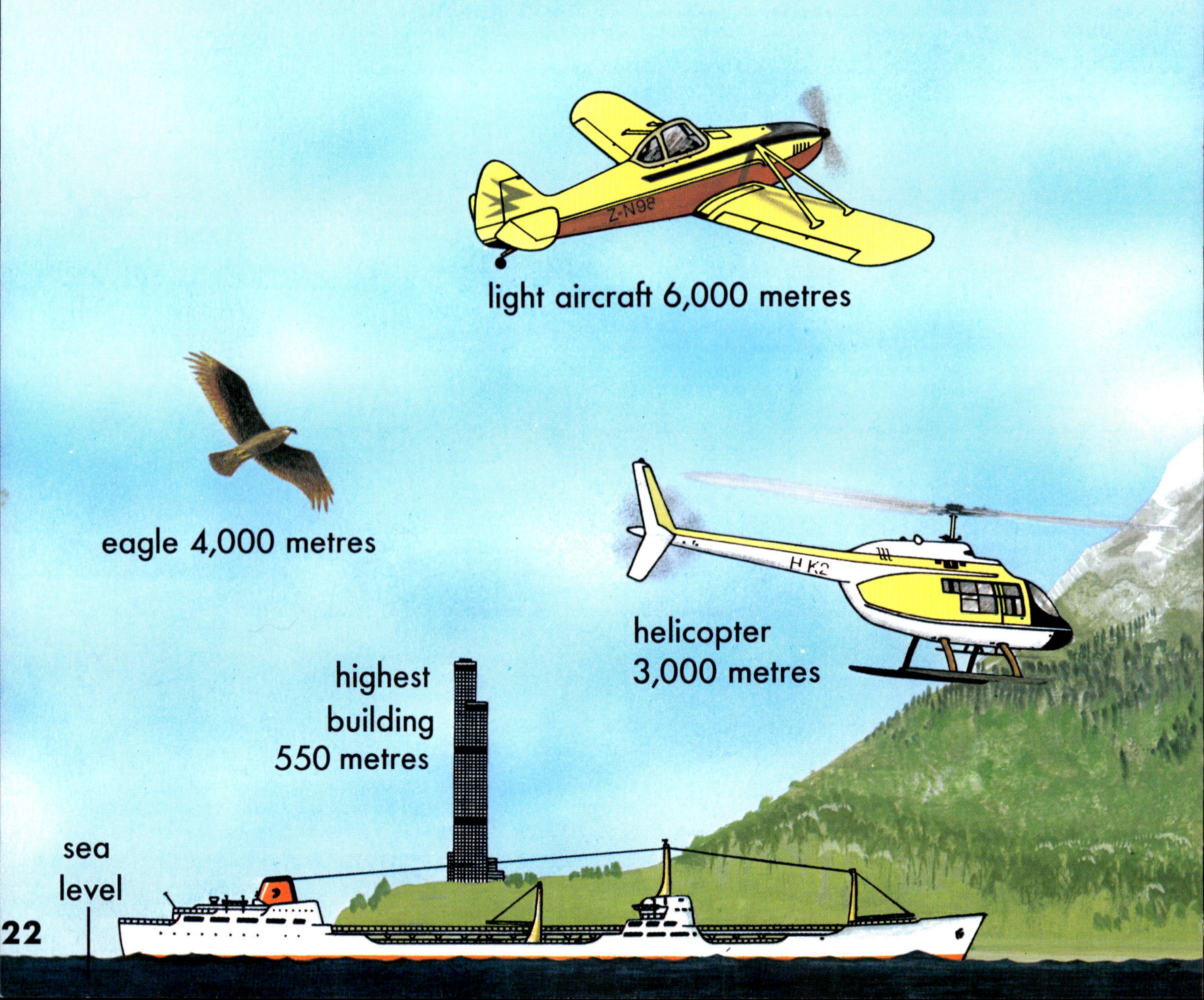

light aircraft 6,000 metres

eagle 4,000 metres

helicopter 3,000 metres

highest building 550 metres

sea level

The water cycle

When the sea is heated by the sun, the top layer of water turns into water vapour. Water vapour is a gas. This gas rises into the atmosphere.

High up in the atmosphere, it is cold enough for the water vapour to turn back into water. Small drops form clouds, but big drops fall as rain. Some rain runs into rivers and then back into the sea. Some is collected in reservoirs for people to use. Some water soaks deep into the ground and then flows slowly back into the sea.

reservoir

Winds

Air rises when it is warmed by the sun. Colder air rushes in to take its place. This moving air is called wind.

Although you cannot see the wind, you can feel it pushing against you. When you fly a kite, the wind pushes the kite upwards. The force of the wind keeps the kite up in the air.

Winds can be very useful. Sailing boats use wind to push them across the water. In the past, windmills used the wind to turn their sails. The sails worked machines that ground corn into flour. Today, machines like windmills are often used to pump underground water to the surface.

Whirlwinds blow round in a circle. Some whirlwinds are very strong and cause a lot of damage. Look at the tube of whirling air in this picture. It is a tornado. Some tornadoes are strong enough to pick horses and cows up from the ground.

Strong winds often bend trees and can break their trunks. This tree was blown down by a fierce wind.

Clouds and rain

Clouds are made of tiny droplets of water or crystals of ice. The droplets and crystals are so small that they can float in the air. Sometimes the droplets come together to make larger drops. These drops fall to the ground as rain. When crystals of ice stick together, snowflakes are made.

cirrus

cumulus

stratus

cumulus

Cirrus clouds are feathery. They form high up in the sky. Rainy weather may be on the way.

Cumulus clouds are puffy with flat bases. Big cumulus clouds sometimes bring heavy showers of rain or hail.

Layers of low cloud like this are called stratus. These clouds often bring rain and drizzle.

29

snow crystals

Snow

When it is very cold, snow falls instead of rain. A snowflake is made up of many tiny ice crystals. All snow crystals are rather like little stars with six points, but each crystal is quite different. The crystals on these pages have been drawn very big. You can see their different patterns quite easily.

The picture on the right shows an avalanche crashing down a mountain. Avalanches may move when snow piles up on a steep slope.

snow crystals

These people are having fun in the snow, but snow is often a great nuisance. It blocks roads and railways. In the picture on the left you can see a train with a snow plough. It is clearing snow away from the track.

Thunderstorms and rainbows

Thunderstorms usually happen in hot weather. Thunder clouds are tall and dark. Electricity in the clouds makes a huge spark, called lightning. Thunder is the noise made by lightning. Long ago, the Romans thought lightning was the weapon of Jupiter, the father of the gods.
The god Vulcan made thunderbolts.

It is easy to tell how far away a lightning flash is. When you see the flash, start counting the seconds, one by one.

Jupiter

Vulcan

Stop counting when you hear the thunder. Divide the number of seconds by three to work out how far away the flash is in kilometres.

Rainbows are made when the sun shines on falling rain. The sun must be low in the sky to make a rainbow. Big raindrops give the brightest rainbows.

When it is sunny and raining, raindrops are like millions of tiny curved mirrors. The raindrops separate the sunlight into different colours and reflect them back.

Watching the weather

It is fun to keep a record of the weather. Look carefully at the sky each day. If there are any clouds, what kind are they? They may be high cirrus clouds or puffy cumulus clouds. If the sky is grey all over, there is probably a layer of low stratus cloud.

You can make a chart to show what the weather is like each day. Draw a sun, a cloud, raindrops and snowflakes on the chart.

To find out the temperature, place a thermometer outside. Look at the number beside the top of the liquid.

You can make a chart to show the temperature. Check the temperature at the same time each day.

To see how much rain falls in one day, you can collect rainwater in a plastic bottle with a funnel.

weathervane

Weathervanes point in the direction the wind is blowing. If the wind changes direction, the weathervane swings round. You could make a weathervane. Use wood for the arrow and post, and card for the ends of the arrow. Put a bead between the post and arrow, and join them all together with a nail.

The television weatherman uses daily weather records like yours to help him forecast the weather.

35

Living in different climates

Houses are different all over the world because the weather is different. Houses in rainy places have sloping roofs so that rainwater can run off easily. Houses in hot dry places often have flat roofs. In cold countries, houses often have thick walls to keep in the heat.

These houses in Switzerland are strongly built to stand up to snow, rain and wind. Some of them have sloping roofs.

In part of West Africa it rains heavily all the year. The ground is often covered by pools of water. The reed houses have sloping roofs. They are built on poles to keep them above the water.

The picture below shows houses in another part of Africa. It does not rain so often here. The houses are made of mud and have flat roofs. The people spend much of their time outside in the shade of trees.

THE FACE OF THE EARTH

Over millions of years, movements inside the earth have pushed up parts of the crust into mountain ranges. Water and ice slowly wear the mountains away. Streams and glaciers pick up tiny pieces of rock and soil on the mountainside. These are carried to the sea. On the way, the rock is often ground into tiny grains of sand and mud.

glacier

hills

lake

cliff

cave

39

Mountains

These peaks are very famous. They are in the Himalayan mountains, in Asia. The peaks were left behind when glaciers wore away the rest of the mountain rock. The highest peak in the world is in the Himalayas. It is called Everest, or Sagarmatha.

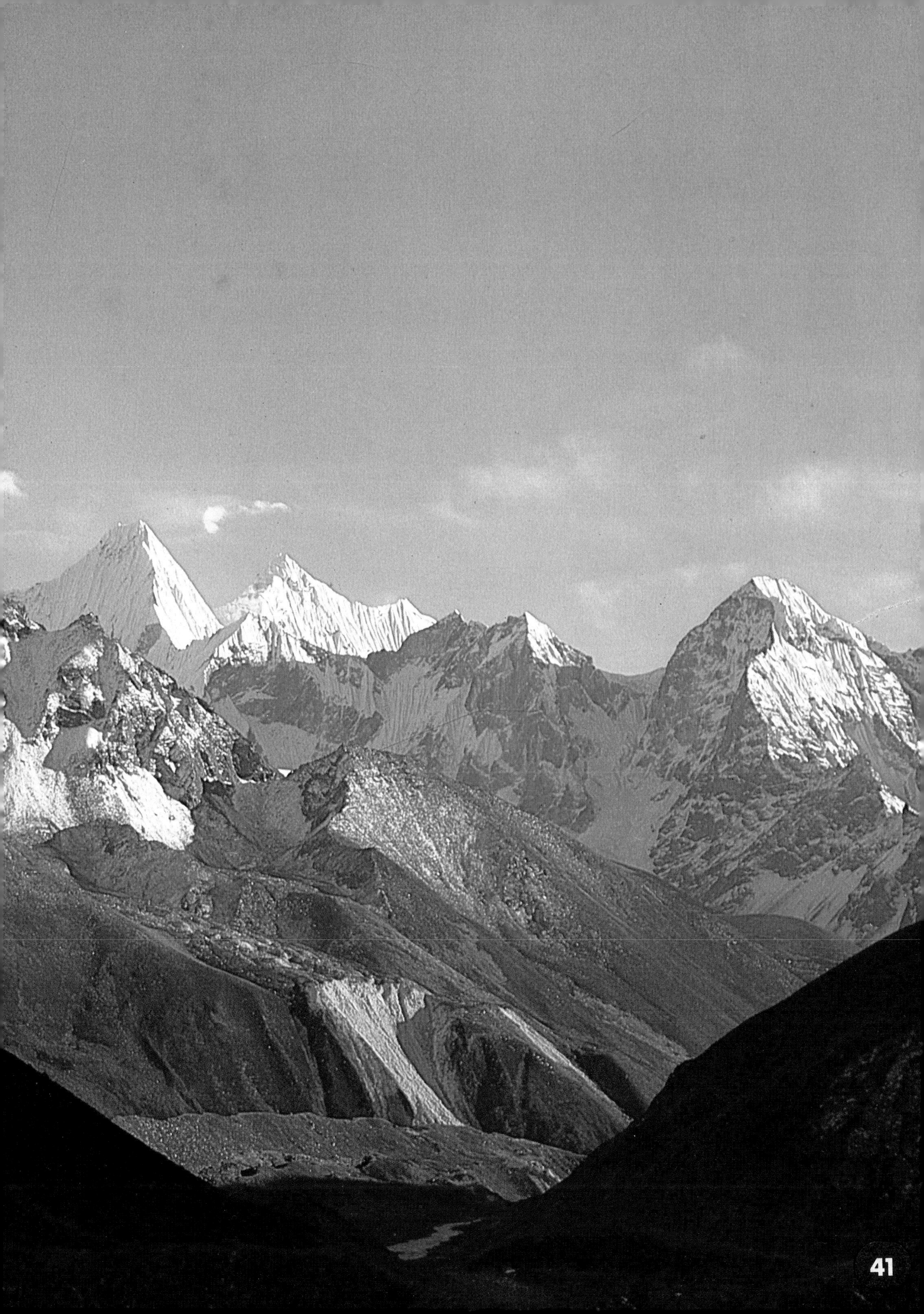

Rivers and streams

Streams usually start high up in mountains, where there is plenty of rain and melting snow. As the stream flows downhill, it is joined by other streams until it gets big enough to be called a river.

The little mountain stream in the picture on the right is fed by water from melting snow.

The river on the right is flowing through a deep gorge. A dam has been built which uses the force of the water to make electricity.

This is the River Rhine. It begins high up in the Swiss mountains and passes through Germany on its way to the sea. Boats carry goods up and down the Rhine.

River Rhine

Lakes and waterfalls

A lake is a hollow that has filled with water. Sometimes the hollow is the crater of an old volcano. Sometimes the hollow is a valley that was made by a river or a glacier.

The water in a lake often comes from a river. In other lakes the water has come from underground.

In Switzerland there are many valleys with beautiful lakes like this one. The valleys were carved out by glaciers thousands of years ago. When the ice of the glaciers melted, parts of the valleys filled with water and became lakes.

When a river flows over a cliff, it forms a waterfall. As the water falls, it breaks up into a spray of little drops. Sometimes the spray wears away the side of the cliff and makes a space behind the fall. In this picture, people are standing in the space behind a waterfall. The space is big enough for them stay dry.

This big waterfall is in South America. The water drops down nearly 1,000 metres to the river in the valley below.

Caves

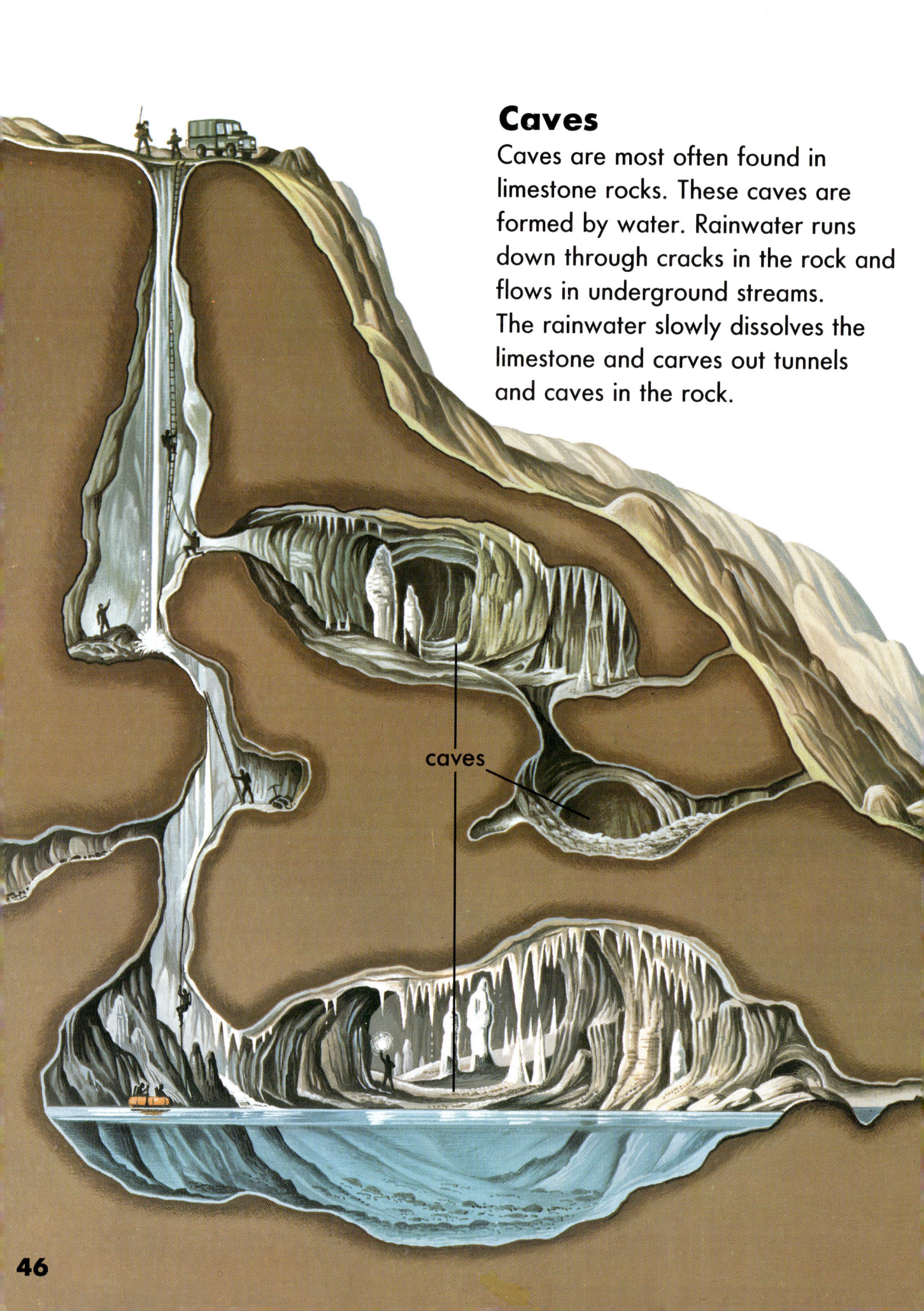

Caves are most often found in limestone rocks. These caves are formed by water. Rainwater runs down through cracks in the rock and flows in underground streams. The rainwater slowly dissolves the limestone and carves out tunnels and caves in the rock.

caves

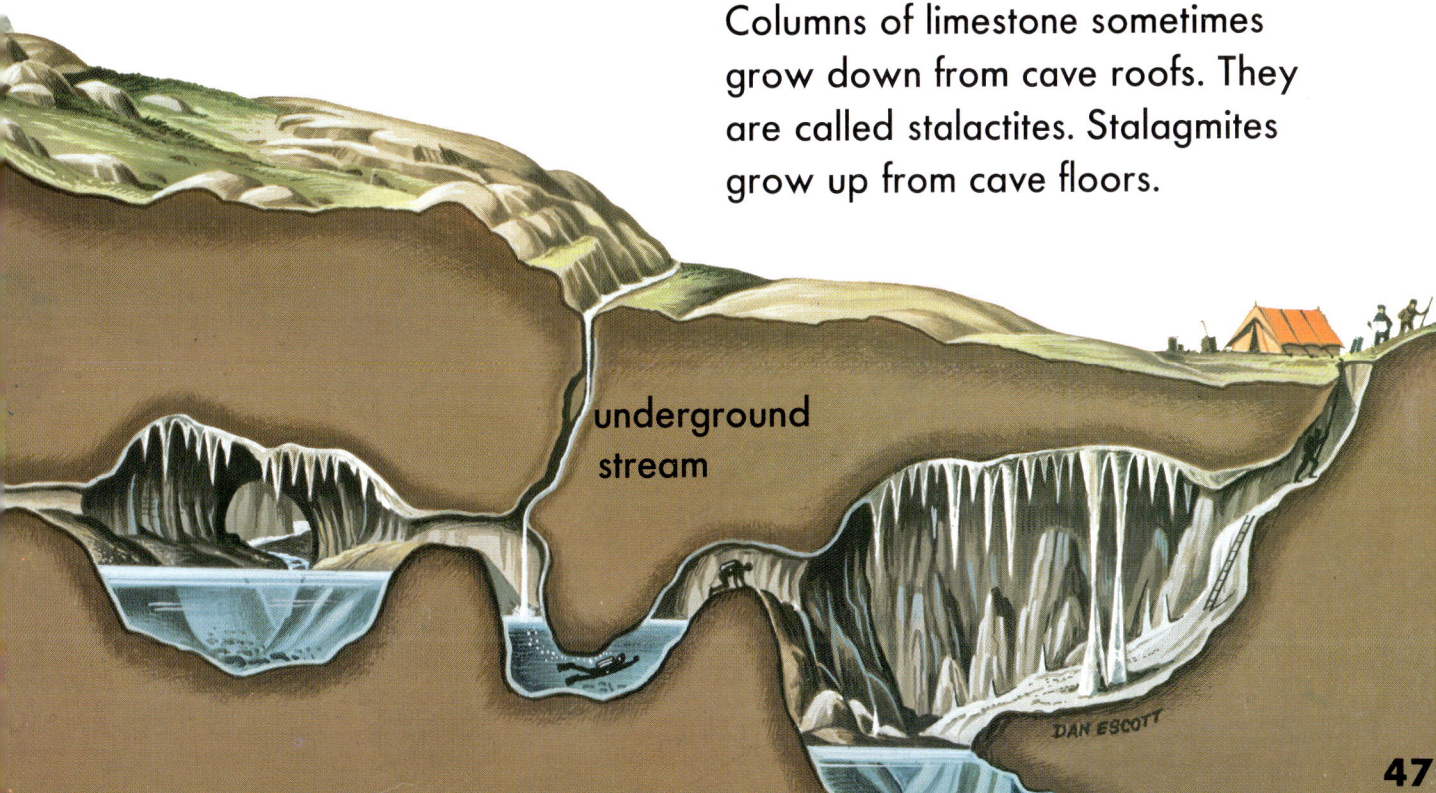

Columns of limestone sometimes grow down from cave roofs. They are called stalactites. Stalagmites grow up from cave floors.

underground stream

VARIED LANDSCAPES

Over most of the earth the rocks are covered by a thin layer of soil where plants can grow. The kinds of plants that grow in different places depend on the weather. Near the equator, trees grow fast and spread into great rain forests. In the Arctic, it is too cold for trees to grow. Only a few small plants can live there.

In many parts of Canada and Asia, winters are very cold and snowy. There are great forests of conifers, trees that grow cones.

In many parts of the world there are enormous areas of grassland with very few trees. In some places the grass grows several metres high.

In some places, rain hardly ever falls. These places are called deserts. Few plants grow there.

In the north of Canada there is thick ice that never melts.

Many parts of Europe and North America used to be covered by forests. Now, most of the forests have been cut down. The land is used for farming.

equator

Heavy rains falls all through the year in parts of South America and West Africa near the equator. Here there are thick tropical jungles. Trees and plants grow very quickly.

Tropical rain forests

Along the equator, the weather is usually hot and wet. It rains nearly every day. Trees of many different kinds grow quickly and form great rain forests. The tree tops are so close that the branches are all tangled together. Plants with long thick stems climb round the trunks. The undergrowth is very dense.

The rain forest above is in South America. The picture was taken from an aircraft. You can see how tall trees of many different kinds grow very close together.

The women in this picture are working in rice fields in Japan. Rice is grown for food in many warm parts of the world where heavy rain floods the land in summer.

Grasslands

In many flat lands far away from the sea, there is not enough rain for trees to grow. Only grasses grow there. Wild animals like antelope used to feed on these grassy plains. Now, sheep and cattle graze there.

The picture below shows a Masai herdsman and his cattle. They live in the high grassland of East Africa. The grass is thick and green because it has just rained.

These plants are all grasses. Emmer and einkorn grow wild. The others are grown for food.

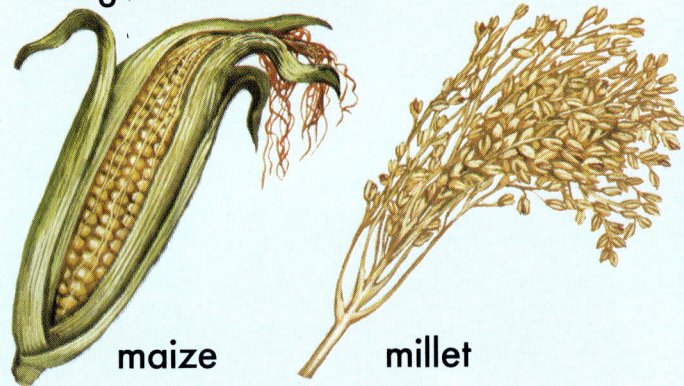

maize   millet

emmer   wheat   einkorn   barley

This is a plain in Hungary where wheat and maize are grown. The horses have been drinking at the well.

A machine called a combine harvester is often used to harvest wheat. The machine separates out the little wheat grains.

combine harvester

Hot deserts

Deserts are very dry places. Only a few plants and animals can live there. It is so hot at midday that the animals have to stay in the shade. At night it can be very cold.

scorpion

addax antelope

fennec fox

rattlesnake

gerbil

The picture on the left shows the Sahara desert. Below you can see some of the animals which live in different deserts around the world. Their bodies have become specially suited to the difficult climate.

camels

pintail sand grouse

desert hedgehog

jerboa

ant lion

skink

Broad-leaved forests

The trees on these pages all have broad leaves. In northern countries broad-leaved trees drop their leaves at the start of each winter. They grow new leaves in the spring. Long ago, great forests of deciduous trees grew all over western Europe. Many forests, like the one on the right, have been cleared for farming.

elm

birch

horse chestnut

56

willow

ash

oak

Coniferous forests

The trees on these pages are all conifers. Conifers grow cones and have needle-shaped leaves. The leaves are tough and can live through very cold and very dry weather. The trees often grow on cold mountains and in dry sandy places. There are great coniferous forests in the north of Canada, Europe and Asia.

Scots pine

larch

cedar of Lebanon

Douglas fir

Each of these conifers grows in a different part of the world. Scots pine trees and Norway spruce grow in northern Europe. Redwood trees and Douglas firs grow near the west coast of North America. Redwoods are the tallest trees in the world. Some old redwood trees are more than 100 metres high.

redwood

blue spruce

stone pine

Norway spruce

Tundra and ice

In the land around the Arctic Ocean, called the tundra, the weather is too cold for trees to grow. Instead, there are low plants like grasses and mosses. These plants grow for a short time each summer when the frozen ground thaws. Arctic plants also grow on cold mountain tops in other parts of the world.

The picture on the right shows people camping in the tundra during the short Arctic summer.

During the long cold winter, the Arctic fox has thick white fur to keep itself warm. Its white colour makes it hard to see against the snow. It can hunt its prey without being seen.

When summer comes, the Arctic fox changes its thick winter fur for a short brown coat. Because the snow has melted, the fox is still hidden from its prey.

This Eskimo hunter lives in the far north of Canada. Here it is so cold that some of the ice stays all year.

Spoiled land

This land was spoiled by waste from mining and rubbish from factories. Not many plants or animals could live here. Then the land was cleared up. Trees and grass were planted. The land was turned into a golf course. Spoiled land can be turned into farmland, too.

63

DID YOU KNOW?

On February 1st, 1839, people in southern England were very surprised to see red rain falling. The red colour was made by dust from the Sahara desert. The dust was carried up into rain clouds. Then a wind blew the rain clouds towards England.

In Japan, some people celebrate the longest day of the year by bathing in iris petals.

In parts of the Sahara desert, there is water underground. Some people say you can go fishing there!

INDEX

Arctic   60-61
Asbestos   16, 18
Atmosphere   4, 22-23, 24, 25
Avalanche   30
Bauxite   16, 17
Broad-leaved forests   56-57
Caves   46-47
Clouds   28-29, 34
Coal   18-19
Coniferous forests   58
Core   8
Crust   8, 10, 12, 14, 17
Deciduous forests   56-57
Deserts   48, 54
Diamonds   16, 17
Earthquakes   10-11
Eskimoes   61
Forests   48-9, 50, 56, 58
Glaciers   38, 40, 44
Gold   17, 19
Granite   15
Grasslands   48, 52-53
Lakes   44
Lava   12-13, 14
Lightning   32-3
Limestone   14, 46
Maize   52
Mantle   8, 17
Marble   15
Minerals   16-17

Mining   18-19
Mountains   38, 40, 58
Oil   20-21
Petrol   21
Rain   24-25, 28-29
Rainbows   33
Rain forest   50
Reservoirs   25
Rice   51
Rivers   25, 42-43, 44
Rocks   14-15
Sandstone   14
Silver   17
Snow   30-31
Stalactite   47
Stalagmite   47
Streams   38, 42-43
Thunderstorms   32
Tornadoes   27
Trees   48, 50-51, 56, 58
Tundra   60
Volcanoes   12-13
Water cycle   24
Waterfalls   44-45
Water vapour   22, 24-25
Weather   34-35
Wheat   53
Whirlwind   27
Windmills   26
Winds   26-27, 35